A Handful of Verse
Volume II

by Misty O'Brien

Nature's World

To he who loves sweet Nature's world
And loves to be alone
Let every bud that is unfurled
Be called his very own

Dedicated to everyone
Who has ever loved, lost
Or laughed!

A Dog's Life

Whether I pad along the path
Or I bounce along the shore
From May until October
I'm not welcome says the Law.

For though I'm fun to play with
And I wouldn't hurt a fly
My unhygienic habits
Might cause somebody to die

And building fancy castles
From sand and stone and shell
Won't be half so pleasant
If my mess was there as well

So although I miss the Summer sea
And beach life in the sun
There're other places I can go
Which can be just as fun

And winter walks I welcome
With kids and Mum and Dad
When sea and sands remind me
That a dog's life's not all bad!

And the Clock Ticked On

She was born today at twenty past eight
With Grandma and Grandpa at the gate
Pushing and shoving to get there first
Grandma hissed and Grandpa cursed
And the clock ticked on. . .
"If she's white, she's mine!"
Whispered the Cook. . Giving the butler
A withering look. .
"Maybe she's black. ." pondered the maid
Mentally counting what she'd be paid
And the clock ticked on. . .
Then silence surrounded the assembled crew
For now it was going on twenty to. . .
And the foal was standing
Patchy, but brown,
Which wouldn't fetch anything
Down in the town. . .
And the clock ticked on. . .

David – Drama Tutor

A tender man, a gentle man
A man of hidden depths
O yes, he's all of these,
And yet. . .
He's also so much more. .

I look upon this man
This dramatic, overt being
Quizzically, uncomprehending,
For I see a dichotomy
A spirit, torn in two. .
By convention? By a loved one?

I hear his voice.
I see him speak.
I know of where we stand.
And yet. . .
Throughout history
Throughout the world,
His spirit feels and sees

A burning city
A war-torn isle
A baby, newly born.
A ghetto and a mansion,
All have touched upon his soul.

He speaks of academia,
He talks of clever men.

He mouths the words of others
But his spirit won't give in. . .

He takes us back, through tragedy,
To taste a victor's bowl.
He watches us plan comedy
And act as children do. .
But where is he? The man within. .
Where has he journeyed to?

A far-off land, where pain is kind. .
Where loved ones, still are free?
Where history repeats itself?
And all of this I see. . .

So look upon yourself my friend
And try to understand
Not all the world is cynical
Not all you see are hard. .
And you, like Life, are Precious. .
And more, much more. .
So rare.

Destiny's Bond

They'd met before, this boy, this girl
Way back when Time was young
They'd forged a bond that held them strong
Upon which their love was hung

They'd talked before, they'd walked before
They'd held each other tight
They'd kept the world around them out
Content their love was right

Then when their love had run its course
And Time, their bodies aged
The bond they'd forged was wrapped in dreams
And ephemeral mists, and caged

But Fate, with smiles upon her face
Once, watching Time for sport
Found our pair in earthly realm
And ready to be caught

They did not know it then, of course
They'd had no fear of Fate
The boy and girl had strode through life
With their own unhappy mate

Blissfully apart they'd lived
Each trying hard to cope
Believing Life had let them down
And working without hope

Then strange coincidences, Strange
Though feared not by girl nor man
Began to shape their destiny,
The paths they trod began. .

To merge and mingle, Friendship grew
The boy, it seems was sad
The happiness he'd worked to keep
Was slowly turning bad

The girl was lonely, hurt and weak
Her heart was broken too
And so the pair re-forged the bond
That Time had wrenched in two

The boy had gathered friends around
In desperate need to ease
And soothe the pain of broken dreams
His conscience to appease

The girl was glad he'd chosen her
To be among those few
She felt at once a stronger girl
And thought the friendship true

He needed her, he wanted her
To stroke his ego clean
He made her feel attractive
Young-at-heart and seventeen

For the girl was more a woman

Middle-aged and far from free
And the boy was young and lithesome
Fair of face and tall as tree

Yet the bond that Time had severed
Was stronger than the years
And the ages, faults and vanity
The half-truths and the fears

And it slowly healed together
Though the pair still didn't know
And the separate lives of boy and girl
Remained the status quo
But the friendship that had started
As a need by both concerned
Began to change and deepen
Into something that had turned. .

Not into love, for Love's too strong
And cheapens what they felt
But into knowledge, shared by both
That no matter how Life's cards are dealt

That each would know, and be there
Like a bond of family blood
To provide support, to trust, to help
To stem the deepest flood

And the unknown bond between them
That was forged before they met
Would keep them close in spirit
However wide they spread their net

For the absences they suffer
And the separate lives they lead
Will not destroy their friendship
Or dilute their inner need

For the boy will just continue
In his search for what he needs
And the girl will keep on hoping
To find orchids 'mongst the weeds

For though the friendship flourished
And there's trust and knowledge there
The pair want different outcomes
One to love and one to care

So the two will ne're together be
Though strong the bond will grow
For the selfishness of both of them
Means diff'rent paths they'll go

And thus we leave this boy, this girl
To go their separate ways
Though Destiny determines
That true friendship lights their days.

Epicentre

The shockwaves that caused the
Dino demise
Ended with Man.
Is that wise?

Closer to the start of disaster
Is the desire of Man to be the Master.
Earth and Life must to him bow
To subjugate the here and now.

But what will be the planet's last request?
Will we remain the uninvited guest?
When our Star subsumes our rocky Earth
What will die, and what will be rebirthed?

Far From The Land

1st verse from Thomas Moore (1779-1852)

She is far from the land where her young hero sleeps,
And lovers are round her, sighing:
But coldly she turns from their gaze, and weeps
For her heart in his grave is lying.

She smiles at them all and offers her hand
And they kiss it with tender care
But her eyes hold no sparkle, her cheeks, although tanned,
Are washed with her tears and are fair.

They know she is grieving, but do not know why
And they try to stop her from crying;
But in front of their eyes, she bades them goodbye
And they realise too late, she is dying.

She slips back in time as she slips into sleep
She's content now, and far from this land.
In peaceful repose, she's beside her love, deep
And she's holding his heart in her hand.

Friends

I know what I should say to you
I know what I should do
I long to hols my arms out
And try to comfort you.

But I also know I'm not the one
Who should be loving you.
There's someone else, much closer
Who you love, and who loves you.

But your love's love is wounding
For your eyes are dark with pain,
And your words reveal the scarring
As you argue once again.

You make it sound like some small game
But games get out of hand.
And what you both get out of it
I just don't understand.

I love you both so dearly,
Can't you see it hurts me, too,
To watch the constant war you wage
In all you say and do.

From Half an Acre to a Window Box

There's half an acre in my head that just won't fade away
And as I tend this window box, strong memories hold sway.
In this aubretia, small and dark, another blue I see
As I drift back through years and tears to find a younger
me.

I well recall a blue-bell'd wood, like giant leafy towers
Where roots and leaves and twigs and earth are carpeted
with flowers
And oft I hear a lover's song as May glides into June
And though the words are not so clear, I can't suppress
the tune.

I peer at grass through misty glass but have to turn away
For behind my eye, it's tall and dry, and gathered in for
hay.
There's yelps of glee and laughs and squeals, the air is
Summer warm
A sudden breeze whips past to show a shapely, youthful
form.

Then like a snap, the vision's gone. I'm staring at my blooms
There's no-one here apart from me, imprisoned in these
rooms
I only have these four white walls, my window and my box
So as I tend this patch of earth, my memory unlocks.

I'll nurture plants all Summer long, and into Autumn's flame
Until this window box and that half-acre are the same

And I am buried underground, though don't be sad I'm dead.
I'll simply become part of that half-acre in my head.

Haiku

If ever a dawn
Were less auspicious and clear
It was last New Year

His Love

He shows his love of colour
When the flowers bloom in Spring
When the butterfly and ladybird
And parrot spread their wing.

He shows his love of Summer
When the sun smiles all day long
When trees display their finest green
And corn and wheat grow strong

He shows his love of Autumn
When the leaves begin to fall
When the fruit is ripe for picking
And there's wine jars in the hall.

He shows his love of Winter
When snow lies thick and light
When sky and earth is white by day
And Jack Frost plays at night.

But he shows his love is perfect
When I hold a baby near
When tiny hands grasp tightly
And a smile breaks through the tear.

He shows his love is passionate
When I hear lovers talk
When hearts and eyes are full of joy
And love lights up their walk.

He shows his love is powerful
When I kneel down to pray
When I need him, he's strong and true
And shows his love each day.

It's Christmas Time

It's Christmas time. . .that time of year
When shops are bright with sound
When preparations cheer the days
And cards and gifts abound

When Winter's at its dreariest
And trees are bare and stark
When gloomy are the short, chill days
And the long, cold nights are dark

So light the candles round the tree
Pour mulled wine in the jug
Open heart and soul to love
And give a friend a hug!

Ice-cream and flowers

With parasol and ice-cream
Tots stroll, in sun-drenched heat.
Each 'Ooh' and 'Ahh' and 'Look, Mum!'
Makes heart and soul complete.

For a child sees natural beauty
In Summer's golden glow
As she smells the perfumed sweetness
Of the flowers in a row

Adorning every window
And in baskets by each door
With leaves of every shade of green
Stretched down towards the floor

Where carpeting each garden
Are rainbow coloured jewels
And pale beneath the apple blooms
Float lilies in the pools.

For a child sees only beauty
As she licks and drips ice-cream
And she stops to smell the flowers
In her perfect, scented dream.

Joshua

With innocence and wisdom there
He looks up at his world with sparkling blue
And a love close nestled, now laid bare

He challenges with cheeky stare
His tempers are a sight to view
With innocence and wisdom there

His words are few, yet spoke with care
With a laugh that grabs the heart from you
And a love close nestled, now laid bare

He often cuddles and kisses with flare
Is happy to tumble and learn from you
With innocence and wisdom there

He toddles and topples, I know not where
Is independent and helpless too
And a love close nestled, now laid bare

So turn away now, if you dare
For those of his calibre are very few
With innocence and wisdom there
And a love close nestled, now laid bare.

London is Full of Women

If Lowestoft is full of artists
And Hoxne's full of treasure
And Sutton Hoo's a sovereign's rest
Then it's difficult to meaure

Should wealth be weighed in history
And not a balance sheet
Then lucky are the Suffolk free
For wherever one like to meet

There's always archaeology
And nought for us to fear
And if London's full of women
Then I'm glad that I live here!

Lost Friends

It's hard to think they'll never be
And never walk and never see.
That you can cry and they cannot
That you will grieve and they will not

But what you are and what you do
Are made from what they meant to you
And remembering what made them "friend"
Will make you stronger, in the end.

Lynn

She's wandering back, thru well-trodden words
To a land where the plants, the fauna, the birds
Are so pretty, and cunning, and wondrously made,
That unlike the memories, they will not fade.

Back to the world she knew as a child,
Where orange and banana and mango, grow wild,
Where sea and sand meet with brilliant hue,
An island world that I never knew.

Now the traveller in her, that brought her here,
Halfway across this Earth so dear,
Is calling again, to countries new,
Where the grass is greener, the sky more blue.

She craves new adventures, new sights to be seen
Wider horizons, a less static scene.
Her message is clear, those closest can see,
Like a captured songbird, she longs to go free.

Millennium

Moulded from and by a star-burst boom
Illuminated by solar light, with atoms of acid and alkali
Lubricated by water and gravity's trail
Landscaped by solar winds and lunar pull
Evolving life-forms begin to cover its expanse
Naturalising naked rock with lichen
Nutrient for an atmosphere of Nitrogen and Oxygen
Invertebrates appear, the arachnid and the gladioli
Utopia for the gnat, gneiss and gnu
Mutilated by 'higher' mammals at this, their second
recorded millennium

Millennium Dome

Some thought it was a dreadful thing
'Monstrosity!' they said.
'A monumental waste of space!'
Complaints from a to z.

Built of new materials,
It grew with record speed.
Pioneering – dominating
It filled an unknown need.

But the common people loved it
They flocked there every day
To see the People's Palace
Of glass and iron and clay.

They watched. They played. They visited.
They walked. They sat. They stood.
They marvelled at exhibits
That proved their life was good.

But then in 1936,
A fire destroyed the dream
And the Crystal Palace was razed to the ground
It's riches no more to be seen.

So when you hear about the 'Dome'
And you think what a waste it will be
Remember history repeats itself
And it might be another 'CP!'

My Love

In a way
I'm glad you didn't stay,
Though surely that seems strange
For you to hear.
But an abject misery
Produced by the chasm left behind
Created another me.

Hot, unwanted tears
Brought regrets and anger to the fore
And did nothing to relieve
The yearning ache,
Or fill the empty coldness in my arms
Or in my bed.

The sounds of others laughing
Trills bitterly within my throbbing head.
Pains and aches are twisted
By the dark, the loneliness, the hour,
Into screaming stabs of wretched agony.

And you?
While all this misery surrounds me,
What of you?
Cosy. Content. Complete.
The missing link within his family's chain,
The last remaining jigsaw piece,
Dropped neatly back where he belongs,
To paint another scene within his life
Upon a mural of existence

That barely registers
My presence there at all.

But worlds revolve
Another day is dawning,
And a smiling sun, and glad companions
Deserve the other me
That loving you
Created at the start.

Numbers

There were lots of them upon the floor
And sliding down the bathroom door
And all of them were sick, or dead
Spewing green, or spewing red

The newsman spoke his words in vain
Within the tv's flat-screen frame.
The warnings came too late you see,
For all at number 33,

"Numbers of sightings now confirmed..."
Droned on the newsman..."Houses burned...
In the western side of town..."And then
Well, the War of the Worlds began again. . .

Parted

O sweet one!
O songbird!
O lark of the night!
How I wish you were here
Next to me!

To touch you!
To hold you!
To see your sweet smile
Is all that's important to me!

I long for the touch of your
Hand upon mine,
The sound of your voice
In my ear.
O how I miss
That tender-sweet kiss
And those arms tight around.
O my dear!

O darling, please tell me
You feel just the same.
O tell me, my love's not in vain.
I want you to say
That you missed me today
And will do so, til we meet again!

O when will that be?
O please make it soon!

You're breaking my heart,
Can't you see?
I need you so badly
I love you so madly
O I wish you were here
Next to me!

Perspicacity – or What's in a Name?

"McCavity!" young Susan cries
With admiration laced with sighs
But better, sure, for cats that see
To be labelled "Perspicacity!"

For mental depth and feline guile
Is obviously part of Pussy's style
Discerning to the nth degree
Would be our "Perspicacity"

Another here loves Baudilaire
And quotes his lines with learned care
A lengthy name, I must agree –
But think of "Perspicacity!"

With penetrating mental thought
A poet conjures art from nought
So future readings, Mark, could be
A page from "Perspicacity!"

Now on to Grammar, Laurie dear
To be correct and please the ear –
If we mean lucid clarity –
The word is "perspicuity"

For "picuous" is not the same
And "Picaciousness" is wrong in name –
But prefix "Pers" – its clear to see
The depth of "perspicacity"

And Bert, with northern Suffolk charm
Who reads his verse with gleeful calm
I'd like to hear the way that he
Interprets "Perspicacity"

As farmland horse, or foaling mare?
As war-time bombers out to scare?
As cosy hearth, with warming tea?
It's all in "perspicacity"

But Michael here, who reads a lot
And always seems to know what's what
Personifies, you'll all agree
What's meant by "perspicacity"

His offerings are short, I know
But depth of thought within them glow
And penetrating? Obviously,
It's down to perspicacity.

Carolyn is Michael's mate,
So Reeder, too, must be her fate.
But twixt the two, both you and he
Have cornered "perspicuity"

For you are blessed with clarity
With which to share with us, what he
Deep Thinker as he well might be
Finds hard in "perspicacity"

Ian Robb with artful pen

Is only half with us again
For half he's left behind you see
With Mrs Perspicacity!

A camera's view's what he holds dear
But celluloid's 2D, and sheer
So photographs, however gracious
Can't be described as perspicacious

Lew's a man who can't be rude
Being a "d" short of being lewd
And musically, I'm sure that he
Exudes with perspicacity

His scores are deep, and so's his voice
He hides his feelings too, by choice
So all in all, it's clear to see
He suffers perspicacity

And Gilly, dear, not least but last,
Before we eat this great repast
With quiet smile you bridge a cavity
With perspicuous perspicacity.

Positive Aspirations

"I yearn to learn the art of singing"
Cheeps the chick of Nightingale.

"When will I cry, haunting, sweetly?"
Clicks the fat and loving whale.

"Who will hoot the loudest, fiercest?"
Pecks the fluffy ball of Owl.

"When you've grown, prepared and practised!"
Stalks the stuffy Guinea Fowl.

Rock Pool

It's a portrait of the sea
Framed by rock.
With simmering, sun-lit eyes,
Through fern-green silken locks.

Pebbles, smoothed and colourful
Are the flesh,
A sea-anemone, the nose,
Soft ripples make a hair-net's mesh.

The ears, two crabs, tucked hidden,
Standing guard.
Courting Shrimps move the lips
Once full, through pout, to hard,

Then fingers, poised above
Know it's strange,
But, touch the watery glass
And by doing so, change.

September

It's harvest time, a happy time
A time of wine and jam
Where fresh fowl hangs in farmyard barns
And fresh-smoked smells the ham

A time of vibrant changing hue
A time of wind and rain
When Summer's flowers turn to fruit
And darker nights fast gain.

And e'en though Winter's close behind
And leaves fall thick and fast
The warmth of cosy hearth will help
Me dream the dark days past.

Sweet Fantasy

O wondrous man!
O sweet delight!
Who comes to me in dead of night,
In dreams and waking fantasy
And thoughts so bold it can't be me!

I dream of him and think him near,
With eye so bright and voice so clear,
With stature tall and arm so strong
He fills my heart with cheerful song.

With trembling joy and yearning ache
I wish him close when I awake,
But dare not reach and bring him near,
For fear the vision disappear!

Summer Froth

Winter wipes the landscape canvas
Drapes the fields with downy cloth
Causes winds and rain to wash them
Whips up storms with thunderous wrath

Though Spring is cleaner, clearer, kinder
Cold winds still need warming broth
Summer's slower, soft and simpler
Painting all with coloured froth.

Suffolk

There's a county here in England
That's a joy to all who know
It's a place of natural beauty
Where the wild and free can go

So come to Suffolk, Stranger
Come feel the East wind blow
Stand on land twixt sea and sand
Forgets those cares and woe

For holidays are peaceful here
The pace of life is slow
Where the work's in farms and fishing
And the rape and beet fields grow

Where the Summer's long and lazy
For the badger and the crow
While the otter and the beaver
Work to keep their status quo

And the land is ever changing
For the rain clouds, dark and low
Fresh keep the green of hedgerow
And ensure the rivers flow

And the coastline washes beaches
And there's sand between your toe
And the east wind, fresh and salty
Makes your cheeks and fingers glow.

Suffolk II

We're bordered south by Essex
To Cambridge in the west
We nudge our way to Norfolk
Yes, but Suffolk is the best

We work the land, respect the sea
We play, we laugh, we rest
We do the same as others
Yes, but Suffolk is the best

We've winter storms that flood the land
And winds that need a vest
We've hail and snow as others have
But Suffolk is the best

When sunshine lights the waving rape
When baskets burst with zest
When field and farm and garden glow
Then Suffolk is the best.

Tables and Chairs

They were sitting at a table
On wooden kitchen chairs
Sighs and smiles and glancing.

They were sitting at a table
On folding garden chairs
Loud music and dancing

They were sitting at a table
On benches, not chairs
Pub grub and attention seeking

They were sitting at a table
On comfy armchairs
Quick smiles and children shrieking

They were sitting at a table
On hand-worn leather chairs
Grey sighs and hand dancing

They were sitting at a table
On wooden kitchen chairs
Sighs and smiles and glancing

Take My Hand

Take my frail and frightened hand
And guide me to the door
This afternoon our worlds divide
And I am so unsure

Yes, take my hand and take my love
Take all your heart desires
Take all the dreams you think you'll need
For all Life's maze and mires

Please take my pale and trembling hand
And guide me down the aisle
This is the time to separate
And we need strength and style

CHORUS

Now take my hand and stand aside
A new man stands between
You give away the woman
But keep the child unseen

CHORUS

I know your eyes are full of tears
Your throat is choked with pride
As you now walk behind me,
Towards the sun outside.

Tell me Why?

Tell me why you passed my way
And why you had to go.
Tell me why you changed my Life
And why I love you so.

Tell me what you're thinking now
And tell me what to do.
For I just do not understand
Why I think of you.

Tell me when you'll come again
And ease my tumbling heart
Tell me when I'll see your smile,
Never more to part.

Tell me where you're going to
While you're so far away,
Who you're with, and what you do,
Without me every day.

Tell me why I feel so sad
And why I sit and cry.
And most of all my dearest love
Please, can you tell me Why?

The Christmas Tree

With forest scent I fill the room
With soft, warm glow I light it.
With trinkets, bells and candles tall,
With baubles round, I bright it.

With twinkling tinsel wrapped around
With ribbons, bows and garlands
I'm dressed in red and silver, bold
Against the green of far-lands

My roots are dry, my needles loose.
My boughs are heavy laden
But I stand tall beneath my crown,
A beauteous white-winged maiden.

For this is where my year is made,
As winter days short darken.
I'll soon be back in Winter snow,
The bright Spring dawn to harken.

The Letter

Dear Laurie wrote a letter
A letter to a friend
It was the kind of letter
Only Laurie dear could send

It didn't say "I love you"
"Get well soon", or "Au revoir"
It didn't relate the dramas
Caused by owning an old car

He didn't sign it "sweetheart"
Or end it with a kiss
No, the gist of this sweet missive
Was this and only this. . .

If 'Mystery' were the topic
Instead of 'Mystical'
Then the focus for this evening
Would have been less spiritual

It would thus be not so difficult
To explain or understand
And we'd find more rhymes pertaining
To the topic on the stand

And he's right of course, I checked it.
So maybe we were wrong
To choose an ethereal topic
To last all evening long.

So if you've suffered for this subject
And have only found a crumb
Then we'll change the theme to 'Autumn'
QED. The questions done!

And though I sign this poem 'Misty'
I'll end it with a wink
For the inspiration's Laurie
And he'd smile at that, I think!

The Shipwreck

What men sailed upon the sea
One calm and sundrenched day
To catch some fish for supper
From the vast beyond the bay?

What thoughts were in their weathered heads
As they sailed far from shore
And climbed and cleaned and cared for
And messed and moaned and more?

What prayers were said, unanswered
To which deity, unheard
When wicked winds and waves combined
To drown each desperate word?

What longings, dreams and destinies
Were clutched beneath the waves
And dashed and drowned or left to die
Within these gloomy caves?

What cries of anguish and despair
Were heard when news reached home
And family and friends were told
'All perished 'neath the foam!'

The wooden planks are rotted through
The rusted nails shine gold
The painted name has long since gone,
The air is still and cold.

And far away, above the roar
Of wind and wave and bird
From beyond the bright horizon
An answer can just be heard.

'We were fathers, brothers, lovers, sons
Who sailed to sea that day
We dreamt and talked of long lives lived
And we had no time to pray.

We were none of us, posh-lipped and perfect
Workmates and friends, that is all.
We were none of us wanting nor wishing to die
Yet we met without question, the call.

So thank you kind stranger, for asking
We all met our fate, to a man,
But you're still alive and lively it seems,
So go live your life, while you can!'

The Plan

It was a simple, ideal thing
A thought that grew and grew,
Nurtured deep within her head
A secret no-one knew.

It stayed there, growing stronger
With every word she spoke
The thought became an embryo
That suddenly awoke

The warmth that spread around her heart
Confirmed the thought was sound
A valid plan began to form –
A partner must be found.

The obvious choice was questioned
The secret dream was shared
Rejection now would mean the death
Of all she'd planned and dared.

But as she verbalised her plan,
She swiftly came to know
That some-one else had shared her dream.
The plan began to grow.

Outside the safety of her head
The secret now, no more.
Supported now by two ideals
It's maturity was sure.

War and Peace

What is war? What is peace?
Would one without the other, cease?
Can we define what makes a war?
Is it oppression, or power over poor?
When will the natives restful be?
And like the animals come to see. . .
That killing each other for War or Peace
Will only make the people cease.

Wheels

Wheels are interesting things
They're shaped like plates, or lids, or rings
They're made to roll on tracks and roads
To help move big or heavy loads.
But that's not all – oh no – there's more
From space to ground, from sea to shore.

There are fat wheels and thin wheels
And wheels in between.
There are wheels that are red
And wheels that are green
There are small wheels and big wheels,
Fancy and plain
There are wheels you see once,
Or again and again.

There are wheels made of cardboard
And wheels made of food
There are wheels made of plastic,
And metal and wood
There are wheels made of stones,
In mills round about
There are wheels that are inside
And wheels that are out.

There are wheels that go round on a bus
Or a train
There are wheels that come down
On an aeroplane

There are wheels used for steering
A boat or a car
Wheels that go short distances,
Wheels that go far

There are wheels that are dangerous
And might do you some harm
You mustn't go near any wheels on a farm!
There are wheels that you play with
And wheels that you turn,
There are even some wheels
That spin round as they burn!

There are wheels in a watch,
And wheels in a toy
There are wheels that bring pleasure
And wheels that annoy.
There are wheels that are squeaky
Or creaky, and croaks
There are wheels that have tyres
And wheels that have spokes.

I could go on for hours,
There's lots more to tell
Like the wheels you can make,
Or the wheels you can sell.
But I'll finish this poem, just as it begins. .
Wheels are interesting things!

What We Like

There's a smidgen of greed
In stating what we like
Whether it's a sunny day
A good meal, or a bike.

In fact its ego-centric
And I'll leave it to our Spike
To tell us all the ins and outs
Of saying what we like.

Printed in Great Britain
by Amazon

28806483R00036